INTIMATE LETTERS

INTIMATE LETTERS

THE INVISIBLE WORLD IS IN DECLINE

BOOK VII

BRUCE WHITEMAN

POEMS

ECW PRESS

Copyright © Bruce Whiteman, 2014

Published by ECW Press
2120 Queen Street East, Suite 200
Toronto, Ontario, Canada M4E 1E2
416-694-3348 / info@ecwpress.com

All rights reserved. No part of this publication may be reproduced, stored in a retrieval system, or transmitted in any form by any process — electronic, mechanical, photocopying, recording, or otherwise — without the prior written permission of the copyright owners and ECW Press. The scanning, uploading, and distribution of this book via the Internet or via any other means without the permission of the publisher is illegal and punishable by law. Please purchase only authorized electronic editions, and do not participate in or encourage electronic piracy of copyrighted materials. Your support of the author's rights is appreciated.

Library and Archives Canada Cataloging in Publication

Whiteman, Bruce, 1952–, author
Intimate letters : the invisible world is in decline. Book VII / Bruce Whiteman.

ISBN: 978-1-77041-212-5 (PBK)
Also issued as: 978-1-77090-618-1 (EPUB);
978-1-77090-617-4 (PDF)

1. Title.
PS8595.H47515843 2014   C811'.54   C2014-902595-5
C2014-902596-3

Editor for the press: Michael Holmes
Cover design: Natalie Olsen
Cover image: Natalie Olsen
Author photo: Neil Flowers
Typesetting and production: Lynn Gammie
Printing: Coach House   1 2 3 4 5

Purchase the print edition and receive the eBook free!
For details, go to ecwpress.com/eBook.

MISFIT

The publication of *Intimate Letters* has been generously supported by the Canada Council for the Arts which last year invested $157 million to bring the arts to Canadians throughout the country, and by the Ontario Arts Council (OAC), an agency of the Government of Ontario, which last year funded 1,793 individual artists and 1,076 organizations in 232 communities across Ontario, for a total of $52.1 million. We also acknowledge the financial support of the Government of Canada through the Canada Book Fund for our publishing activities, and the contribution of the Government of Ontario through the Ontario Book Publishing Tax Credit and the Ontario Media Development Corporation.

PRINTED AND BOUND IN CANADA

For Ken

"He is the other half of my heart."

— Horace, on Virgil

TABLE OF CONTENTS

I   INTIMATE LETTERS

    FOUR LAST POEMS | 3
        IN THE MAGIC CIRCLE OF NIGHT
        OF YOUR SCENTS AND BIRDSONG
        DREAM-RAPT AT DUSK
        THE GARDEN, MOURNING
    URGENCY | 9
    BEAUTIFUL HUMAN TRACES | 10
    ELEGY | 12
    AT PÈRE LACHAISE CEMETERY | 14
    SANE INTREPID FORGERIES | 16
    LOVE POEM | 17
    BREATHING TOGETHER | 18
    THAT RECOLLECTED MUSIC | 19

II WRETCHED IN THIS ALONE

BARE RUINED CHOIRS | 23
HER ABSENCE FILLED THE WORLD | 24
IF THE DAY WRITHES, IT IS NOT WITH REVELATIONS | 25
YOU MAKE ME ALONE | 26
OLD DESIRE AGAIN RUNS THROUGH THE BLOOD | 27
MY LOVE WAS MY DECAY | 28
UNENDING MISERY OF AN UNALTERABLE WORLD | 29
DEATH BY MUSIC | 30

III MUSIC TO SLEEP IN

AFTER SPICER | 35
INVISIBLE GHAZALS | 39

IV DESIRE

DESIRE | 59

ACKNOWLEDGEMENTS | 64

I

INTIMATE LETTERS

IN THE MAGIC CIRCLE OF NIGHT

". . . im Zauberkreis der Nacht"
— Hermann Hesse

Mountains ring paradise. The sun is still on its tether. Sloughed roof tile in a red clay pile.

Late afternoon light and wind ripple the pool water. Leaves high in the air blow left and right. A pigeon plummets like an arrow onto a stone.

Immigrant palms flex their green muscles in the bright air. Black shadows come and go. The cat darts self-consciously at a lark.

All directions of the compass congregate in a small circle at the tip of a peaked roof. The air bites its own tail up there. The weathercock is still.

The incontrovertible logic of night is still far off. It lies in a dusty unlit corner where the wind and the sunlight are moot. It is a hummingbird's tongue, barely noticeable.

Something unseen chitters high in a tree. The wind picks up and muffles its odd vibrato. Traffic noises counterpoint that voice.

Your dress lies in a red circle on the grass. Bees hover over it, glad for colour. A single mourning dove sits like a whole note on the telephone wire above.

Stones ring a bottlebrush tree. Two cactuses rise like pillars in the grass. Almost everything is green in the yellow light.

The desert outside these greeny walls is stark. Dark stones and pallid sand stand endlessly repeated into out of sight. Slight chance of any redemptive moment.

Human objects intervene. A brown chair with three slats at back sits slack at a table. Lime pieces float in a plastic glass.

A spindly tree rises out of the back patio. Your splayed body sleeps quietly on the bed. Out of doors, a slate table sits empty.

Night descends finally as the elliptical sunlight fades. The vibrissae on the trees go still. The room fills with soft grey air.

The desert night is old, cold, silent now that all the planes are grounded. Now is not the proper time of month for moonlight. The cat skulks by, hunting now for fellow tetrapods.

The desert night surrounds this place with an intimate clasp. Lights like eyelids open up and barely penetrate the dark. The arc of "nothing there" creeps out from under trees.

The desert night inspires faith in stones for comfort. They are hard things, immovable, not prone to deception. They go dark before the dying light obtunds.

The desert night envelops every passing car. Their dust and ruddy lights are fast wiped clean. They fade from sight in no time flat.

Shadows grow like grey chalk on the orange wall. They are a second reflection, evolving and elusive like a poem. They pulse and sway and finally are erased.

Shadows mass and quiver behind seven tall trees. No less real than green fronds, they shiver and fade at dusk. A single streetlight casts its listless pall.

The wind picks up at five o'clock. Everything not near to the ground despairs and cranes its neck to live. Darkness lies around that special corner.

It is the wind brings the magic circle of night. Lovers bide their time and wait amidst piled blankets and feathered berms. Love is enough whether they sleep for a while or not.

OF YOUR SCENTS AND BIRDSONG

"... von deinem Duft und Vogelsang"
— Hermann Hesse

Away from soap your hair smells deep with the promise of skin, the place where our bodies abandon their silent grief and containment and spill out onto each other.

Love wants to live at the cutting-edge where light and hair declare their inefficiency at self-definition. Something lasting like the sound of birds agreeing to flee from high waves and salt spray, inland to sun and sweeter smells.

DREAM-RAPT AT DUSK

"... nachträumend in den Duft."
— Joseph von Eichendorff

All girlie domestic things deserve my love and rapt attention.

Damp underwear hung in the shower stall and the smaller V-shaped half of a bathing suit crushed into a corner of the sink. Disencumbered hair let loose to float in darkened underwater rooms. Fortunate islands of books with their intimate signatures and menstrual histories.

A Chinese box holds sox that lie like piled cordwood.

THE GARDEN, MOURNING

"Der Garten trauert..."
— Hermann Hesse

A crow works hard to flap aloft, perching on the soft, enormous bloom of a high tree. The garden is full of dirt, colourless as the sea and dank after days of rain. The lemon tree is hung with haphazard fruit, hard as stones, and red holly berries stain the grey air. Dissolving in the intermittent sun, rusty furniture reminds us that the garden is only for this morning and not forever, whatever that is. Grapes and roses will flourish and die, nourished by the dirt and the rain slanting in from the sea.

We stay inside and watch the garden indulge in its slow grief. Our slow embrace has nothing of heartbreak in it, for all that it elicits the smell of unknown flowers, suddenly in the room. Of course bereft of much that went before and cannot be recalled, we still get deeply by, counting on the present. All birds and flowers after all are starry messengers arrived just in the nick of time to save us from regret. Our slow embrace has nothing of regret about it.

URGENCY

"Wie himmlisch schläft von meinen Blicken
Die schöne Welt"
— Johann Mayrhofer

Even in the face of trees that will outlive me, the world seems beautiful. The quiet sun beats down on me as well, and on raucous wretched cars bound for the scrap heap, on nimble cats nine times game for risk, on impassive books of useless infinite poems. It lights up ageless rocks that line the street and bugs that come to life and die in one day's compass.

Every small-town psychic knows that the greatest urgency is to live inside the moment. Death is there too but barely visible. The rectilinear shaggy bark of a mesquite tree dries and falls off one bit at a time, inside a slot of present time not all watched over by ugly fate. Fate itself is beside the point to the hot green towel flung carelessly over a bit of outdoor furniture, or to a nameless bird pecking fecklessly at an ancient chryselephantine cactus near to collapse. His urgent mechanical beak finds sleek slivers of something resembling food there, while what's around the corner stands still.

What paradise the world seems, laid out before my gaze. Time, which only lately feels like a predictable emergency, drifts off into a post-orgasmic sleep. As Cicero said, life is all mind and appetite. They both bear doubly down and make their fierce demands, patient and happy in their own sweet way. *Eunt et iuncti sunt.* All the senses vie for equal time: liquid sunlight, forestry of an arm's hair, a motet by Rameau as natural as sheep, sweat under a lover's arm, eyelids closed in bliss.

BEAUTIFUL HUMAN TRACES

"en nuestra cama de la luna"
— Federico García Lorca

The prospective inviolate heart wants love and a simple life: work that is desire too, cadmium yellow sunshine, cats leaping at invisible motes in the morning air.

Love simply pervades the house. It spills from the shower as you wash your hair, alphabetic, and commanding, and full of truth. It wafts from your clothing as you move from room to room, penetrating to the corners and rising as light as air. Love alights in your wake as irrefutably as a chair. Every sacred and domestic object has its scent.

Poetry and music seem to speak of little else. A chant by Szymanowski slants unpredictably into love's ear, and a piano trio by Haydn, wordless, too. Love is obsessive or love is nothing at all. Poets winkle it out from any unlikely thing, russet fruit, earnest wimple, rumpled emotions of all kinds in a hopeless heap. Cavafy's sweet voices echo in the distance like music, voices of the dead that live still in love and poetry. Stevens's missed revelations, laid bare and beautiful as daylight, are perfectly accessible to love. Crane's consanguinity is remembered and revived and kept infinite in a kitchen cabinet where cats sneak in to play with plastic bags.

Naked bodies rest quietly on the bed that love surrounds, determined that the future should fête their blind devotion. Nothing tests their love like the complicated indurations the past invokes: family tithes, remembered erotic sighs, whatever envelops the gestes of long ago, other personages, and crass events. Naked bodies forget the fetid past. Naked bodies live to promise vested inexorable pleasure.

More than other body parts toes leave historical traces. Everything else happens in the erotic air. Fair kisses fly like birds across the room. History stares senseless from the corners while caresses test truth: wide-eyed, full of commotion, utterly open-hearted. Caresses become part of a permanent story recorded by the human heart.

ELEGY

For my mother, Marguerite June Whiteman (1917–2006)

"Pain wears out like anything else."
— Marge Piercy

You died after dark, within near memory of spring's equinoctial turning, past sundown, snow still on the ground. You simply ceased to breathe, as though pleasure or fear invisible to the rest of us had suddenly caught your heart unawares. Your body lay still but seemed as deeply attentive as ever. The hard breathing, wrenched from somewhere buried deeply beneath the bedclothes, a reverse sigh that meant you would not willingly let go, could not last one further pulse. Death and winter conspired — and your soul was gone, just like that.

Everything around you stayed the same. The floodlit hospital room did not go dark. Rocks strewn at the side of the parking lot did not rive or shudder. Undramatic death stole a march on your heart while your children blinked. The feverish plink of blood at your wrist shut off, and your clenched fists gently went limp. If there was a moon that night it shone unmoved.

The girl you were died too and something in us all, living because you lived: juniper and tamarack in winter on Mount Royal, nerdy thirties movies, two oppressive nine-foot Steinway grands, between which you sang your heart out in Sieglinde's guise. *"Du bist der Lenz,"* I wrote on your winding-sheet, shy to evoke the occult past when nothing that did not speak the present seemed right. Death is not an end, but it plants the crucial moment hard into our lives, those of us who go on after.

You told me once that music equalled sex. Only later did I realize that you blushed at saying so for another reason, that in fact you had traded music for love in a grim bargain and were sorry for it at times. They always intersect no matter what we say or do, however sadly Tristan dies and leaves Isolde passionately game for death when love has gone away. Those famous lovers called into your life once, and beautifully you passed their passion on. *"Ich liebe dich"* of Grieg and Schubert's "Crow" were like a bridge, from fifty years ago to now, when you and I said yes irrevocably to everything they stood for: love, of course, remembrance too, the certainty of future doubt laid bare. Music accompanies every distant act and makes it sweet, or tries.

Sad preparations for you, a daughter of the sun like every woman. That sun shines now into my western-facing window, declining on the sea but beautiful, a living terror to the ragged cat that jumps at it with blind abandon.

AT PÈRE LACHAISE CEMETERY

At Père Lachaise the invisible dead swirl in silent clouds beneath the earth. An unseen raven squawks its peevish note, five times, before it stops or flies away.

It's spring, and the grass and trees have put out shoots with no embarrassment or sense of shame. Death among the famous, now and then, continues to mean nothing to the green world.

Yet the dead command the ground outside of time. Their monuments decline and crumble in the wet air, rust and fall in shards, mixing sexually with the dark earth and the relentless greeny weeds. Their painted names cannot resist the sun and rain that sweep them, in slow motion, into oblivion, bereft of anyone who cares, even finally bereft of human thought. Names constructed over centuries rot and disappear inexorably, multipliers of bodies but no less consigned to intimate yellow dust.

It's spring, and handsome birds are everywhere, honking and whistling and singing, casting minute shadows on the crummy alphabet of human perseverance. The cemetery fights to keep its self-definition, to resist the canonization of raucous birdsong: strut and bourdon and amiable flit. The irresistible birds seem to say that love is now, and nothing matters more; not testament of any human manufacture, contrived song or traces of a paintbrush, rooms encumbered with torpid books. The rook sits still and formulates a feverish prayer, wordless as desire, as commanding as the afterlife of the happy dead. It caws at heaven like an idiot, caustic and ignorant of earth, cognizant of air and nothing else.

The famous dead remain interred, for all that reverential fools still clamber on their bones. They know better than to ask for more than passing tutelary affirmation, a momentary glance from an unconscious creature. Love perdures and they do too, in wondrous silence, like the rhythmic sun through intermittent branches of a tree, stationed over tombs: Chopin and all the silent, demonstrative dead.

Outside Père Lachaise the *motos* fart and briskly switch from lane to lane, self-confident as stars and ignorant of death. Somewhere on the radius of earth, Chopin speaks, drowned out by the grossly fecund engines of despair, whisked aside by capillary noise, silenced by an orchestra of birds; yet still he speaks from underground, and lives.

SANE INTREPID FORGERIES

The heat bugs cry at noon, unseen in the tracery of green leaves shimmering against the sky, but there, like poetry is there. The wind renews its intermittent shiver. An airplane passes invisible overhead. The thick impasto of the air is always there, like poetry is there.

The sound of the cicadas flickers like a sprinkler, a little sine wave of what there was and what's to come. Flies forage on the wooden fence, buzzing and shutting down at random. The gravid moon is somewhere, sheltered in the blue corona of the sun, awaiting revolution.

Shadow and light adore a pygmy jade plant, green and cream astride a terracotta pot. Root and branch hoist it up and into the afternoon air, trembling at its farthest edges over white paper swamped with light. Poetry interrogates the day and all its luscious store: glimmering ice cubes in a plastic glass, swimsuit hung athwart a tree, semen drying on a rock.

And poetry goes from there, game for anything, crazy for distraction. It fills up like a metal tub, forgotten out of doors, with leaf and branch; a dumb arithmetic of loam. A hurricane lamp protects a silver flame. Imagining it is easy. Just write it down. Poetry drips like a white stain down the side of a galvanized tub.

LOVE POEM

The rain will not stop. It flows noisily overhead and it hums like a low cello note. "What a relief it would be," Spicer said, "to give all this up/ and find surcease in somebodyelse's soul and body." All this is rain on the roof and poetry, flowing like honey heated. Down here the slick world fades into grey and the rain pools in the street as clouds gather underfoot.

Your body is farther than the rain away, naked or not but always naked really. An unholy landscape is what lies hard between us, water rushing over mud, decaying snow at 10,000 feet, lost time. How foolish is it that I fly like a dumb bird south and not east into your body's sacred geography. How foolish is it that the rain capers down the beaded glass, and the whole world tapers into a small windowless room. Loneliness is a windowless room in a blackened building. All over Berkeley the lights have gone out.

BREATHING TOGETHER

"This does not change.
This does not change."
— Ralph Gustafson, "Winter Solstice"

It does change, Ralph, it dies.

The ordinary vision of love in the backyard — watering flowers or raking leaves, clearing a path from house to snowy road — disappears through no one's fault. It doesn't take evil, heavy-handed men to kill love, just time's slow melt from then to now. Love had nothing to do with loveliness in the garden. They perfectly coincided for a moment and you thought to write it down.

Breathing together, heart to heart, blissful in bed or gazing through glass, everything collides. The world you move through, Love, and make your own is my world too. The Tchaikovsky Trio that fills the room is water we both float in, silent where you are, across the table from me, yet imagined against all odds.

Press yourself against my chest and sigh.

THAT RECOLLECTED MUSIC

"I dream because I wallow
In the unreal river of that recollected music."
— Fernando Pessoa, "Un Soir à Lima"

We translate the past again and again, trying to get it right. The translucent rhetoric of dream and poetry's white light get partway there. Love too reminds us of lost moments and diminished time, the future (I'll love you forever) dislodging what's forgotten: a creek, say, expressly frozen for hat tricks at dusk amid a symphony of adolescent whoops; or sofa cushions bound in yellow worsted, cracks between them in simulation of a girl, made passionate by the secret use of boys.

But it's music that penetrates every recollected hour, the piano kissed by a frail hand in charge of memory's lure. Precise invaginations where music fills the empty space of thought, thought which peters out and dies as fast as a change in the weather. The sun will rise on another day and last night's lucubrations melt and be despised. But at 3 a.m., roused by the need to pee or by dream's outlandish demands, music takes hold of the dark: Mozart, Mussorgsky, or Martinů spins melody like a man bereft, or a ghost under orders. The dreamer, or he who wakes in music, cannot withstand the tune's commands, almost to delirium. All time seems to be under music's evanescent fate, a little bit of what madness irresistibly is.

II

WRETCHED IN THIS ALONE

Quid sum miser tunc dicturus.

"What shall I say, miserable as I am?"

Dies irae

BARE RUINED CHOIRS

I speak to no one and no one speaks to me.

It's barely light, and the swollen river in early spring, choked with dirty melted snow and whirling Styrofoam, runs by out the window. No sweet birds sing, though ducks with flickering wing keep rushing by. The unleaved trees assault the sky in vain. They don't give up. I do.

"Her absence filled the world," an artist said. Yours does. Cruel imposing memory is all I have, thinking of you then and missing you now like air, like whatever else I cannot live without. I cannot live without you's the horrid truth. I think of your frozen hair, swept after swimming by a winter wind into a sudden nimbus, or your warm feet notched into the bedclothes next to mine, unconscious as we were all night, resisting praise. The thought of you raises Saint-Saëns' final sounds to plink in the silent air around my hurting head.

It's bound to be forever brown outside the window. Losing you I've lost it all, spring and every nascent thing it pushes into my silent life. Love goes on but has no further force except to hurt. It stains the future brown. Love runs away like slow indifferent water. Loss wears my empty heart away like rain.

HER ABSENCE FILLED THE WORLD

"... And you and love are still my argument."
— Shakespeare, "Sonnet 76"

We took the great breath of lovers but now we breathe alone, and incomprehensibly your body in the world is pain. Consolation drifts out of reach like music in another room, barely recognizable before it goes *tacet*. I don't know what to say.

Eros-the-loosener-of-limbs has no advice. Permanent loss is not in his lexicon of love. Language itself is a machine that has swallowed an alien object and cannot go on. It will always be wet and silent out of doors, like Christmas Eve, with the moon in its first quarter coverted behind the clouds. Mute cows haunt the gloom beyond the city. They love one another and never leave. I don't know what to say.

The Persian lovers sing of wanting the bond of love to last forever. It doesn't. Mad, intolerable determination snips it to drag on the muddy ground. It flops uncontrollably, spurting heart's blood in the air. Enough blood for lost love can never be spilled. I don't know what to say.

Your absence is everywhere. I see you disappear from all our sacred places, beds and other blessed furniture, rooms with no discernible geometry, sunny lawns and other implausible spaces made holy by your loss. Well, no. They were always holy is the truth.

I don't know what to say.

IF THE DAY WRITHES, IT IS NOT WITH REVELATIONS

A crazed soprano sings that love is cruel, especially when it is offended.

How can unrequited love emerge from love requited?

It shouldn't work that way.

Selfish thief, you took everything back and locked it away: five years of my life and all my love.

Your perfect talent for hurting men goes on.

I hurt.

YOU MAKE ME ALONE

"Du machst mich allein."
— Rainer Maria Rilke

There was a time when every poem came to life in a visionary recital of love. Your body kept me incandescently alive. The taste on my tongue from your fingertips was bliss enough for days. Now I am alone because you made me that way. You drew up a list, red-checked what was missing, and bundled me off on an airplane. I'm the fragrance that left no trace behind, the wind that rustled in the corn and then went still.

You go on with your life alone. Your body carries twin fish from place to place. They are always with you. You look to your rituals: food and sleep and dress, you know? I imagine you every day at these things. The cats purr and you brush your hair and you keep me away, day after day. The snow melts and the trees turn green and you keep me away, day after day. The fish grow bigger and you keep me away, day after day. I suckle rocks and trees and gamey-smelling glass bottles, because you keep me away.

Yeats said: "Man is in love and loves what vanishes. What more is there to say?" In dreams I put my arms around you and you vanish into air. Once, hectically, you drove a car and I wound up with my luggage on the side of the road, running vainly after your disappearing taillights. The valises fell to bits and my clothing flew away. From the backseat, later, I lectured your parents on the word "phallus." Clearly I'm losing my mind.

I'm losing it because you made me alone. My days are all knells and lintels and elegy. I owe a line and more to every unknown sweet face met in the street, and all the lovely objects of my life. They crave repute and recognizance. I'll have to save it 'til *tristesse* subsides, and all the pretty flotsam of the day contrives to have its say again, even if I'm alone.

OLD DESIRE AGAIN RUNS THROUGH THE BLOOD

You changed everything, twice. Never was abandon so sweet in the first place. It was so, you said, delicious, to be horizontal at last. We left so much behind that day, foresworn to history and happy neglect. Kisses have so little underneath them. Everything is coming next, wholly unmixed emotions and leaps at forever.

No, forever is forever out of reach. The days go by and soon the past is our past, double-edged and full of snares. Is love less love when storing up resent? Desire never stops running through the blood, or so I thought. Wrong. Abandon was never meant to last.

The circle closed in stark abandonment, but love cannot desist. I am powerless to get you back.

MY LOVE WAS MY DECAY

O there are no more words to write. Your spirit walked away, taking love with it. I say your name a hundred times, praise its tetragrammaton as though speaking to heaven itself, but it does no earthly good.

The ocean is out there somewhere beyond my ken, hard to bear in its constancy, too far finally to give me hope. Magic is dead and I cannot willfully make your dear body appear, even in mind's eye, to hold me dearly up. I am deep in it, hurt, worthless word.

The worst was this: love.

UNENDING MISERY OF AN UNALTERABLE WORLD

Your spirit walked away and the world seems waste. Not death cut deeper, sweet forever you, not any living thing. My bloody heart craves living in the past, full of your scents and ten bright toes, the days all orange and rapture. It was unacknowledged prayer to trust your love, but prayer as always proved profoundly false.

I had never enjoyed the trust of — what? — the world, but no sooner had you let me kiss your lips than I was swallowed whole by some ecstatic way of life. Mad solitary being, you calmly took possession of my heart. Rote bliss banished woe.

Dream the world and make it over. No, it never really changes by a fleck. Not a spot of heaven stays alight, determinately try as lovers always do. There's only hell, really, in the aftermath of impatient you.

DEATH BY MUSIC

The headphones clung to his scalp like a kell, as Mozart's final music poured into his unlistening ears. Eternal light wasn't at issue. Death is a dead end always. He lay there rigid and no longer able to speak, wrung from life by the loss of love and organ failure. No need to guess which one.

III

MUSIC TO SLEEP IN

AFTER SPICER

"Music to sleep in"
— Jack Spicer, "Orfeo," *A Book of Music*

I

Orpheus presumably lay in the open air on a *lektron* of ground cover good for a few eclectic hours of bourgeoning sleep. His *cithara* would rot in the humid night air if he lived long enough. One night he dreamt prophetically of driving in a car with Eurydice at the wheel. Technology is so much more easily imagined than the heart's future. He broke down in tears and upon being asked why could only say, "I don't know. I don't know." Eurydice, wearing a chauffeur's cap and ruby-red lipstick, began to sing, "No more grieving, no more dying, o my life, o my heart's treasure," the right consolation from the wrong opera.

The cat called Grace is licking its paw and cleaning off the dirt of the urban garden where she sleeps. Her night music is the cawing of crows and the creepy oversight of a television ramped up for a deaf man living nearby. Purple agapanthus guard her fragile body. Cats dream of the screams of mice and wrench themselves awake when noisy rain begins to fall. The garden rots amid pussy thoughts of a dry season.

Freud said, "Even the predisposition towards perversions must not be something rare and special but is part of the constitution that is considered normal." Normal Eurydice roused him out of sleep with morning pee, "half smiling down at nothing" Keats would later say, pressing Orpheus to ecstasy. The music of the everyday begins right then and never stops. Orpheus adds a note from time to time.

11

All men are wretched at saying how lonely they feel. They weep in hotel rooms, jerking themselves to sleep in sloppy queen-sized beds. Sitting naked in the garden the day before his wedding, Orpheus is alone amid threatening flowers and dangerous honeybees. Sweat and the hot sun curl the hair around his nipples. He thinks about poetry and its inability to push back the dark, its mute admission of failure. No one wants its astute rhythms, no one lives or dies by its stark recognitions. Nail polish and mockingbirds, silver rings and *helix pomatia* matter more. Poetry makes no one less lonely, thinks Orpheus in his white plastic lawn chair. His lanky cock lies flaccid along his flank.

Orpheus imagines a wedding day full of jacaranda and bougainvillea, champagne and recitative. All through the night men and women will dance with each other, then fall into bed at dawn. It will be June, and during the ceremony the purple and red flowers will drift down in the wind. *S'agapo*, darling, they'll whisper to each other, after standing up amidst poetry for the conjunction of souls.

III

"Heal/Nothing by this music"
— "Orfeo"

Drunk with definition and self-assertiveness, Orpheus capers in a stranger's backyard and squawks like a cock at dawn. He's lost everything but doesn't know it yet and hears sweet melody in noise. The wedding's off. Eurydice's in a silent lonely car bound for nowhere, unhearing out on the Nebraska flats.

"I am the big bird," Orpheus thinks to himself, "the little birds should remain quiet and let me sing. Eurydice's the now-you-see-her-now-you-don't kind of lover, but she stays in my life when the music sounds. I should sing all the time and screw sleep. Sleep is for the unloved. We have our relentless music to restore us."

INVISIBLE GHAZALS

"I wait for a word, or the moon, or whatever,
an onion, a rhythm."
— John Thompson, *Stilt Jack* XXVII

1

Is it still possible to say with Yeats that everything we look upon is blest? Anyone can die alone out of the sunshine and bereft of love, love that sings in the bones. What intolerable late night pain it is to fall asleep alone like a stone marking nothing at all. The complicated grief of dream's investiture leaves the dreaming lover naked as before save for the adornment of the ancient light of stars.

Cars with tremulous passing lights drive by and shore up nascent suicidal devotion. Everything everywhere contributes to the dreariest dark conviction. The dead and undesired cock lies like a stick on the flesh, friable and lost now to good fortune.

It is no blessing that as the weather turns grey, suburban animals disappear into their safe houses, leaving stillness and late-summer leaves to rot in the garden with ill-tended fruit that long ago gave up.

Tangible misery in the browning trees pressed hard, as though a hundred dying were a hundred fates,

not one.

2

As summer dies the ragged unbeautiful roses and their emergences grow hard and likelier to wound. Balls fallen amidst them stay to rot. Broken ineradicable toys resist extraction and focus the waning light.

All human objects abandoned in the world seem odd, chords without resolution, sticks caught on gluey rocks in a stream that comes and goes beneath a shiny rain. They rest there like desire, feckless and a little loony.

A lovely idiot cranks his fucking radio, forcing a quartet of Debussy into every overgrown corner of the yard. Red leaves rain down like . . . no, not blood, not blood but something warm and wet from last night's dream.

Hölderlin asks where the light is. It always seems to be failing, before or after the equinoctial moment. A piano, left out overnight through drunkenness or sour indignation, fills with snow and topples to the ground.

3

Our undying confidence that the body blesses time makes all bright certain moments brighter still, like music, say like Schubert, two bars in the sweet domestic bliss of — of, oh, what is it, D. 959?

Seven sparrows line up on the roof for food. Seven times a day I miss your breasts so adamantly I could throw myself under a train. The sparrows swoop up and down for hardened corn. I stay stupidly silent, forlorn as a single bird not in the guidebook, from elsewhere maybe, nudged here by global warming. The intangible influence of the weather gets me down.

The clock runs out on poetry. Who's to say the sometimes intolerable sun won't skip a day and stretch our faith to the breaking point? The strain of optimism rests on my chest like a brick.

4

How can a pallid butterfly half-seen on the wing in the brilliant yellow sunshine of a late October day make anyone, even a poet and moral coward, think, "the immemorial tragedy of lack-love"? Oh God forgive me, for ever foisting my shit on other creatures, crows, and cows, and kissing bugs. Carlos Williams intelligently understood that women will not bear the turgid micturitions of stupid men.

Everything in the wind blows one way like the heart, the tick-tock of desire even in abysmal ignorance. It comes (the wind comes) from living an in-between life, not sure of anything save the overdetermined past.

Books pile up like laundry, ready to be recycled. Redemption isn't there. It lies in your long brown hair.

5

The rain and the sun and the passionate steam rising from the morning grass. The maculate grave. Leaves fall to the ground like words of love, words of coming to an end staved off: a penitential silence. They fall to no music at all. Only the wind makes noise. It crawls over the city like a drunkard hitting the low bars.

Ovid in Tomis among depraved shepherds had a ghastly fate. The yellow fat in sheep's milk made him long for Rome.

In early winter a naked oak tree casts a giant shadow over the yard. Squirrels skitter over it, spooked by its black transparency. Dark as the grave wherein John Thompson is laid. Nothing eats at the heart like rain uninterrupted, like love.

6

The rain of March taps hard on the tympanum overhead. This ripe time of year the landscape consumes your soul and gives back nothing. If only all the trees would fall and take out all the houses in this town, yielding Eden. Winter does that, making cruelty seem fetching.

By far the only certain chance at bloody efficacy is booze. The weather's all against pussy, and poetry's a crock. Booze is all that's left.

Even when a passing train and its recondite signal feels like it might be a way out, *out of what*'s the question. We sleep too much or yearn to. Down the line there's only more of same.

I want you, don't you know? The evanescent crap of making every day evoke the next and then the next again makes everybody nuts. Or me at least. I can't believe the shadowless afternoon consolidates the dreams of anyone, leastwise lovers who aspire to something more than unremembering.

7 (DOLOROSA LANE)

Nothing is harder than the silence of your back, your shifting hand dropped from mine in sleep. I hate the hiatus of inconclusive night, of dreams in which I've lost a car or lose my wallet to some faceless mercurial thug. All my debts are of the spirit, it seems. Who can die and be dead and quiet with such a thing hanging over his head? Like Chapter Eleven, death doesn't solve everything. Any bankrupt spirit can tell you that.

I want to take my fleshy finger and write a poem on your silent back, even as the letters form in disappearance, piling disillusion on disillusion, thought untenable on sullied flesh. Solid. You're not listening.

The snow keeps falling silently. It isn't fair. Blowing leaves leave invisible traces on the earth's fair skin made white by winter's slow retreat. Poetry's relentless glare is buried somewhere there outside the reach of sleep.

8 (THE OCHRE MUSE)

Her face makes sense at fifteen feet. Up and close it's just a mass of muddy browns, a mess of feelings. Four scarlet birds in the leafless maple tree out back make me happier, but then they're gone. Fuck it.

What's so glorious about happiness anyway? America overdoes it.

The first day of spring and the muse is full of grief, or maybe it's me and it's just depression and relief that sunshine has a future. Does the muse care about the weather, or about whether we make it or not? What's making it, anyway? She's got it made, I'd say. She owns the world and holds my unsuspecting head in her hands like a piece of fruit or a soccer ball, poised to bless or smash as she sees fit.

Her nakedness is my undoing. Up and close she smells of paradise — if paradise is orange and smells like flesh.

I'm making all this up, of course, with help from her. Nothing banal or almost evil surprises her. She's heard it all before.

9

Late Beethoven overtures, cardinals crashing free-fall into burgeoning bushes athwart the garage, dandelions randomly celebrating the short but sweet life we live: it's hard at times to get beyond the moment, the sensual stuff of every day, Duncan's "familiar comforting beasts in the dark."

I'm foolish and think the dark will keep us safe, happiest drunk and wallowing in your sex, blind and only half a sec from pure redemptive bliss, even if such bliss is only mine, my dear. It's catastrophic when you come because we're done, and I can't learn to love the end. It's too complicit with that other final thing, goodbye.

Out the window birds decide to end it all by kamikaze raids that leave them bruised but ever on the wing, unpredictably hungry for more. They stagger off and who knows where they die. Who's ever found a dead bird in the course of days?

Name day, consecrated house, faithless unhappy girl.

10

Some awful interregnum of the heart is making me crazy. I haven't the least idea where to turn. It's nighttime, there's nothing out the window. The wine bottle's in the recycle bin. I should sleep. The birds and squirrels and every fucking lucky creature on the street has stopped the race for food and sex and found a space to rest, dumb and safe for now. The moon is new, only my light is lit.

My disinherited self is restless amid the quiet gloom. I check the door obsessively for parcels, even after dark, convinced the UPS man is a messenger from heaven. Stranger things are true. Your apostasy, for example. What am I to do with that? I don't believe in God. *Qui seminant in lacrimis* etc., but I'm not sure I trust the Psalmist any more than God. Poetry, with its unintended lies, is little help. What good are words when breathing hurts and all the litter of sixty wasted years lies strewn about and rotting on the floor?

Newfound friend, melodrama, help me out. When poetry fails (it always does), lift my heavy heart.

11

You've stopped consoling me. That's the hardest part. Your feet evade mine in our bed. You obdurately face the other way and think and dream of things I cannot know. Where did you go? The wind stops. The birds fall down. I've failed you.

You seem to think it's fine to set a man adrift. You've done it several times. I'm numbers three and four. We made up once.

The birds are back. I hear them on the monitor while our chirpers sleep upstairs. Grackles, finches, and jays. Straight talkers.

Greying Mike will soon be here to till the garden. Seeds are utopian, don't you think? It helps a little to know what I'll be eating in the fall. Mike lost his brother this year to drink. Everyone has his cross to bear. I don't know what to think. Maybe I'm a baby, needing kisses and babble to get me through the day. It's hardscrabble, life without your unconditional love, your woodwind dreams and uninhibited pubic confidence, unabashedly happy once, you. Where did you go?

Three times a day the train goes by with perfect dedication. The claxon sounds and citizens scatter and someone loses a leg from time to time. It wakes me up at 4 a.m. and makes me think the world's about to end. I can't control my usual resilience to dire fate or the thought of it. The worst part of being alone

is thinking too much.

12

The high wind's long hysterical gusts intimidate me. I come to dread the next one like a birthing pain. It's unbelievable that women still die at nature's crap command. The radio's calling for tornados. The birds flit about intolerably fast and make me nervous.

It was in weather like this that Eurydice disappeared for the second time. Don't look back. Such perfect and such perfectly ridiculous advice. Nobody's listening to me, and I can't blame them. Eurydice probably preferred to put up with the difficulties of hell. No one does your dishes there, or keeps the recycle box clear of empty gin bottles. And what about emotion?

The road to hell is paved with serenity and independence. Never admit to needing another soul. Die first, more than once if need be, by indirection and discounting need. A car, or god, or something stupid whacks you on your blind side and your soul, alone by choice, remains alone forever.

How ridiculous. Fate is what you deserve. Orpheus has a vast repertoire of windy antiquarian oldies. He's always free for funerals.

13 (VARIATIONS SÉRIEUSES)

The arpeggio of wind over an inch of water in the big backyard, and a dozen grackles lurching after easy worms. Their feet cause minor ripples that vanish fast into the stillness. Felicitous morning, even with half of the world drowned. Water seems like the best of the elements to end in if the end must come. Black birds, red birds, columbine, crimson maple trees: everything thrives drunken on its chosen drink. I drink too and watch the grackles lunging after slippery worms. The register of intellect is in their favour.

The wind dies down to nothing and the water mirrors the sky, thick with clouds and passing birds. Adagio variation, a D-major seventh when the sun breaks out. Add a G for piquancy, a melting moment. I want the music to sound forever, but of course it moves on and resolves. Why must everything resolve and move on? Tomorrow, when the water has silently seeped into the ground, the birds will move on for elusive worms elsewhere. I'm inclined to slip into silence too, tired of the high emotion of white women and white men, game for death by drowning, even if it's only an inch.

14

How can I make a poem out of nothing? I'm sick of abandonment. I've had my share. Apparently love is a river that comes to an end. Not enough water remains even to drown in. No one tells you this. Or everyone does. It amounts to the same thing.

Discouraged, dejected, depressed, desolate. One day ends and another begins, after a sleep like death, or dreaming of it, death seductive as a sweet to a sweet tooth.

It's good to dream to get things out of the way. A little nocturnal abandon makes the day begin at nothing, which is as it should be.

1 5

The ant's a romantic in his dragon world, hoisting invisible love on his elliptical head and threading a maze of harm to make it somewhere safe, where love resides, if amazing love resides anywhere. The robin shakes its head a dozen times and hobbles away, uninterested in ants and treacherous love. Love should pervade the world but seldom does.

I cannot bear to think of the past today. Flowers persist in the garden and only unpetal over days. Once they were nothing and soon they will be nothing again.

We live on eyeglass crumbs. Your body isn't for me anymore. It's gone like love, like the animal whose bones I found on the railway tracks. You shower and shut the door.

IV

DESIRE

DESIRE

    For Kiff Slemmons
    "]ιμερω["
    — Simonides

1

A tiny fragment of an
epinician by Simonides
survives on a torn bit of papyrus
found, among many thousands of
similar fragments, at Oxyrhynchus
in Upper Egypt.

How strange
for a single word
without context to be
assignable to a known poet,
alive and appetitive
2,500 years ago,
and for that word to be
himeros, desire.

Many poets, wanting only
a single word to survive them,
surely might choose that one.
It is the carnal opposite of
the heroic, not single-minded at all,
not communitarian, not
something of the future but
of the present, and
thus so profoundly unlikely
to last beyond a poet's death.

Yet desire does persist.

It outlasts Achilles' earthy valour
— blood, cum, sweat in authority,
Hector dragged bloody
around the walls of Troy.
It outlasts Aeneas
shouldering his father
as Troy burned, and
carrying him off on his mission
to found a city, a country, a race.
What is more heroic than that?

"I was trapped in the present,
as heroes are or drunkards,"
admitted Proust's eponymous hero,
Marcel, at one point,
caught as a young man in the
mesh of alcohol, flesh, and poetry.
Desire connects those
deep modes of self-knowledge
and keeps them also in the present.

"Heroes eat soup like anyone else,"
said Jack Spicer in a poem,
and without a shadow of a
doubt, Hector, Aeneas, and Marcel
all ate soup with real relish
and no sense of its being unbecoming.

Jason ate soup and died ironically
under the weight of an antiquarian
figurehead. Odysseus rested in
domestic bliss and the cessation of
hostilities, giving in to desire
after his ten years of hexametric distraction.
Dawn rose in a stripe above the old stockade
as he awoke in Penelope's arms.

2

Joseph Cornell is a ghost. Darwin, Mandelstam, William C. Williams.
Cocteau's erotic long fingers are placing a call out to Glenn Gould.
Colette and Nabokov, lost, need to fantasize sexual splendour.
Lautréamont never died; he envisioned a permanent lost world.
Debussy strangled his deep love, and drowned his desire in war rot.
Never forget even bad poets; they make a difference always.

3

Desire is so prevalent it
disappears from view like
fog or perfect sunshine. We
are surrounded by it always,
invisible as grass or sky,

pervasive in the beds of
heroes where they love and
lie, dying untransfigured but
content with unforgiving death.
They loved harder and felt

pain more. The grain of desire
runs through each of their days like
music, and it ends but is not
forgotten. And
Hero herself, with her

pure white hands and
cinnamon breath,
took naked Leander to her
naked flesh, wet from the
sea, unflinching.

ACKNOWLEDGEMENTS

Poems in this book have appeared previously in *Raritan*, *OR*, *Pleiades*, and *Literary Imagination*. I am grateful to their editors for their support. "The Garden, Mourning" was issued in 2009 as a broadside by Mixolydian Editions, with a wood engraving by Richard Wagener. "Desire" was commissioned by Kiff Slemmons for her book *Hands of the Heroes* (2009).

Wretched in This Alone was published privately as a chapbook by Ethan Lipton in the summer of 2014. The title of this group of poems is drawn from Shakespeare's "Sonnet 91" ("Wretched in this alone, that thou mayst take/All this away, and me most wretched make"). I have taken almost all of the individual titles from other poets, and here acknowledge my borrowings. "Bare Ruined Choirs" is from Shakespeare's "Sonnet 73." "Her Absence Filled the World" is from a quote by William Kentridge in the *New Yorker*. "If the Day Writhes" is from Wallace Stevens's "Notes Toward a Supreme Fiction." "You Make Me Alone" is the first line of a Rilke poem. "Old Desire Again Runs Through the Blood" is a line from C. P. Cavafy's "Return." "My Love Was My Decay" is from Shakespeare's "Sonnet 80," and in fact my piece is a palimpsest on that poem. "Unending Misery of an Unalterable World" is a phrase from William Carlos Williams's novel *In the Money*. This poem is also a palimpsest, on Shakespeare's "Sonnet 129." I am deeply grateful to the Vermont Studio Center for a month's residency during which these poems were composed.

The title of my book has been borrowed from the nickname given to Leoš Janáček's String Quartet no. 2 (1928). This profoundly passionate music was written for a much younger woman in the year of the composer's death.

The author thanks the Ontario Arts Council for a Writers' Reserve grant that helped him to complete this book.